LIGHT and SHADOW

LIGHT and SHADOW

Poems and Reflections

Barbara Letts Blodgett

Barbara Letts Blodgett

ISBN:	Softcover	978-1-5035-1473-7
	eBook	978-1-5035-1476-8

This book was printed in the United States of America.

Rev. date: 12/05/2014

To order additional copies of this book, contact:
Xlibris
1-888-795-4274
www.Xlibris.com
Orders@Xlibris.com
698490

CONTENTS

I. NATURE

II. JOURNEYS

III. LIFE

For my sons, David and Kent,
their wives, Darlene and Lyn, and
seven grandchildren –
Connor, Austin, Bryce, Calin,
Natalya, Adison and Jalyse –
In gratitude.

NATURE

NIGHT

Through the window
A hazy moon,
Appears,
Disappears,
Behind wispy clouds,
        Building,
                building,
Becoming solid.

A strong breeze
Sets the palms thrashing,
The sound,
        louder,
                louder.

Drawn outside,
I want to know it first-hand -
Warm,
        enveloping,
                invigorating,
A tropical night
Near the ocean
In paradise.

EARLY MORNING

A quiet early morning,
Silent, but for the creaking of the house,
        Song of a bird just outside.
Through the window, I see a doe and her fawn,
        Nibbling their breakfast in the pasture.
The rocking chair sits nearby, still,
        The chips on its paint, the worn arms
        Bespeaking its use over several generations,
            A comfort.

This time, precious,
Time out of time,
Outer world at rest,
Inner world calm, full.

I hear your footfall on the steps, your day beginning.
You will go sit at breakfast, drink your coffee.

A shared life, habits of years in the making.

THE PERFECTION OF A LEAF

Order,
The green of it –
          Dark, lighter ribs,
The simplicity,
Its design,
          Even spacing,
Inherent beauty.

A glimpse into the mind of God.

HARVEST

Burnished gold
Land and sky,
Leaves and sunset,
The sun low in the sky.
Leaves falling, flying,
Corn stalks yellow/brown,
Having yielded their golden treasure
For man and beast.

Harvest time, a race against the elements,
Crops at peak,
Prayers for clear weather,
Forbearance of rain,
Offered up by farmers, families;
Long days of heavy work,
Culmination of the season's planning,
Nurture, industry.

Memories of childhood visits
To the family farm,
Uncle and cousins in the fields,
The women preparing a table laden with
Fried chicken, mashed potatoes and gravy,
Green beans, and pies baked that morning,
Cherry, apple.
The men hot and tired from their work, showering,
Coming gratefully to the table and sustenance.

The fields of stubble, cleared of excess,
Neatly tucked away for winter.
Satisfaction of work well done.

In good seasons, thanksgiving
For nature's blessing and bounty,
And a well-deserved respite.

FAVORITE TIME OF DAY

A time of long shadows,
I walk in the early morning,
As the sun makes its climb.
A Kingfisher cheeps as it scouts the water.
Downy Woodpeckers start their tapping
        On a nearby palm.
The sky fills with birds awakened,
Leaving the mangroves
To inhabit their favorite feeding grounds,
Everything energized by the promise of a new day.

THE DANCE

The quiet of an afternoon sail,
Light wind,
        Full sun,
                Water lapping against the bow.
Two small butterflies – black wings, orange markings,
        Fly aboard,
                In and out of the rigging,
A silent dance
And then are gone.

IN A HURRY

Why am I running?
Where do I think I am heading at such a pace?

I go outside.
I stop. Sit down.
Look up.
Cirrus clouds slowly pass above me.
A light breeze blows early summer leaves.

I am here now.
I read a poem.
A quote from Anthony Machado catches my attention:
"Beyond living and dreaming
there is something more important:
waking up."

I wake up to
life, blessings, connection, gratitude.
Where have I been? My eyes, ears, heart, my soul?
Blind, deaf and dumb
Until this blessed moment
In which I float.

HAIKU

Shadows envelop
The languid pool as koi swim.
An old man dozes.

JOURNEYS

Greek Adventure

Rhodes, Crete, Patmos, Delos – islands of myth,
legend, ancient human history, glory,
Heralded for deeds of their gods, their heroes,
fought for and fought over by scores of soldiers,
citizens, numerous ambitious leaders and
nations,
from Odysseus and the ancient Greeks,
to the Romans,
to Suleiman the Magnificent and the Turks,
to Mussolini and the Italians of the twentieth century,
now returned to the Greeks.

And I, a curious, somewhat awestruck traveler,
struggle to take it all in,
while the local inhabitants, inheritors of this trust,
go about their lives,
perhaps only vaguely aware of this legacy,
these special places.
"Bow down, bow down,
appreciate the ground on which you stand",
I want to urge them.
"Live, as I am… living a dream",
as I wander this lovely Mediterranean world,
its lush climate, plentiful foods –
the apricots, figs, almonds, olives,
all manner of delights;
its blue waters, so clear,
its lovely coastlines,
and houses of white.
No wonder so many peoples have wished to possess this land that I feel privileged to visit.

LOVING THE GREEK

On a recent trip to Athens and the Aegean Isles
I fell in love with…

The blue waters of the Aegean, its multitude of
islands, coastlines;
The blue and white of the Greek flag, mimicking the
colors of its waters and houses;
The evidences of history, sense of pride in
accomplishments of long-ago
heroes, kings, leaders, poets;
Archaeological sites exposing the mastery of building in
ancient temples, palaces, homes,
amphitheaters, libraries, water systems and
unisex public toilets;
Beautiful, dark-eyed, dark-haired people, olive
skinned Mediterraneans who roamed
and ruled the seas millennia ago;
Marble – in ancient and modern buildings, wide
walkways, extensive walls in gardens,
interiors of homes and palaces; rooms and
tubs for bathing; foyers; verandas;
The love and development of art evident in ancient
statuary, mosaics, frescoes, friezes, pottery;
Family, its importance and tradition, multi-generation
homes with open floors awaiting the
next daughter/son and family,
Gathering with friends at outdoor cafes
to see and be seen, to visit,
to drink coffees, or wine, or grappa
or raki, later in the day;

Generous, delicious dinners, enjoyed late and long;
The joy and pride of a restauranteur, who, having been praised for a meal, brought extra courses,
a complimentary dessert, pitcher of raki;
Café frappe – mid-morning, with luncheon,
mid-afternoon, any opportunity to sit, chat;
Feta cheese –
In salads, on sandwiches,
Fried, crumbled, melted, in slabs,
For breakfast, lunch, dinner, in-between;
Seafood –
Calamari, first course on every menu,
fried, sautéed, broiled or plain,
with lemon, not tomato;
Octopus, displayed on lines near fishing boats
in the harbors, offered on menus of
nearby restaurants.
Fish (Bream, Dorade), freshly caught,
though less plenteous,
having been overfished,
the generosity of the sea depleted.
Olives of black, rose, green; and olive oil,
delight of chefs and patrons alike,
an essential of Greek cooking;

The Mediterranean…its sensuality….

POW-WOW

Not a Native American, something drew me
        to this gathering.
Having traveled in the Southwest – Arizona, New Mexico,
The jewelry in many of the booths was familiar.
But the drumming, the dancing were a discovery.
Following the sound, the beat,
I entered the huge tent, ringed by vendors selling
        Necklaces, semi-precious stones, herbs,
        Turtle-shell rattles, decorative pottery,
        Suede jackets.
But the drumming, the drumming,
Was insistent, starting softly and
        Growing, growing in intensity.

A tall man stood watching, dressed in native attire.
His head and back were arrayed in eagle feathers,
The beading on his buckskin shirt, intricate, carefully done.
"Your …costume? dress?, is beautiful."
He looked down at me with a slight frown.
"It is called 'regalia'. I am from a northern tribe –
        Cheyenne – in Wyoming."
"You came to Florida from Wyoming for this Pow-wow?"
"I live in Largo now, here in Florida."

His feet started moving to the drumbeat,
        As did all the others.
Little by little, feet stepping, bouncing lightly in place,
The People were drawn into the circle
        Of hard-packed earth
Where they danced individually, but flowed as one,
        In the same direction inside the circle.

Each moved according to his own pattern,
Own personality:
    Young boys in mocassins, randomly,
With unbridled energy, showing off,
    Young men with vigor, intensity,
Proudly inhabiting their native identity,
    Young girls, self-consciously, but joyfully,
Spreading their arms wide, displaying their brightly colored
Shawls, dipping and diving,
    One older woman – an elder – in black and white,
Barely moving her feet, but
    In rhythm, in rhythm,
With such dignity, such composure, that one could not
    Help but follow her movements
    As she stepped, stepped.

Something about this scene, this event,
    Created a profound sympathy in me.
'The People', gathered to celebrate their common heritage,
    Too long hidden,
The distinct identity of each tribe, their ways, patterns,
    Too little honored,
The making of their drums,
    Too long forgotten,
Their singing,
    Too long unheard,
Their dancing,
    Stopped.

Now they gather again,
Re-discovering the richness of the ancestral ways,
    The importance of their traditions
    For themselves, for their children,
    For Us all.

AFTERNOON ABOARD SPIRIT

Whispering
        through
            the water,
Enjoying the motion of our ketch
        gliding on a
            light,
                gentle
                    breeze,

Reading Hemingway's "A Moveable Feast",
        memories of Paris....

Perfection.

NORTHWEST IMPRESSIONS

I.

A jagged dark line of firs, spruce, red cedar,
Against a backdrop of white, shifting to blue,
Interrupted by the snow-capped peak of Rainier…
The Northwest skyline
Cradled by the water of Puget Sound:
An Easterner's first impression of this
Very different landscape.

Then, from the perspective of the water,
Sailing on the Sound,
The wind is calm, the water swirling around us
In confused eddies,
The current strong through the Narrows,
The suspension bridge silhouetted
          Against a leaden sky.
Clouds come and go in great clumps,
Leaving Dutchman's-britches patches of blue.
In the distance, the Cascades display themselves
          In layers, separated by haze –
Reminders of the Japanese landscape near Fuji,
Artists' scrolls, depicting same.
Rounding an island, a puff of wind catches the sail
And we surge forward,
          heeling over.
Though the air is unseasonably warm for March,
The water is cold, our sail a brisk one.
A sudden calming of the wind is welcome,
The sun breaking through, creating a pocket of
Warmth in which we bask, relaxing.

A group of boats engaged in a race appear
At the far end of the Sound,
A picture post-card, but in slow motion.
We are lulled by the gentle rocking of our boat,
        The quiet,
        The deep azure of the water,
        The scenic beauty.

Dinner awaits onshore,
Our reverie now interrupted by the starting of the
Engine as we return to Gig Harbor, sated.

II.
Another day, driving north to Vancouver,
We note the Native American names on
Streets, parks, mountains, casinos –
A tribute to their historic and present-day heritage.
The Cascade range looms,
As we climb and descend, climb and descend.

Passing through a valley where tulips are grown
        By the thousands,
The broad expanse, now bare and brown,
Obscures the dormant possibility of
A patchwork of bright golds, reds, oranges –
A wondrous sight in spring.

Walls along the highway depict
The evergreen landscape,
Dominated by firs, spikes of green.
Beside the road are stands of birches and alder,
Occasional pines.
A large tree split by lightning, lies toppled,
        Having died a sudden death.

Rows of poplars delineate boundaries here,
In contrast to
          Stone walls in New England,
          Split rails in Pennsylvania.

Coming in sight of the Cascades,
I think about how it must have been for the pioneers,
The loggers, the trappers,
Seeing these mountains for the first time,
Considering how they would settle here,
Meeting those that already had made this their home,
Who live here still;
Staking a claim to territory they thought
Free for the taking,
The richness of the minerals, the forests, the wildlife,
Also free for the taking, in their minds.
At what point does our culture recognize the value of
Giving back,
Preserving,
Living in gratitude?

It is a long time coming.

WOMAN ON A TRAIN

She was ordering a vegetarian dinner as we stood
waiting to be seated.
Not paying much attention, we were ushered
to places across from her and her companion.
Conversation on such a trip offers little promise –
sometimes polite, awkward, with no evident
common interest or experience,
sometimes one-sided, one is talked at –
sometimes just silent, with occasional requests
for salt, sugar…
Thus, low expectations.
Conversation began.
Thoughtful questions,
Insightful observations.
Those eyes – intelligent, alive – gazed back, causing
a second look,
real engagement.
What is responsible for such energy, depth?
Diet? Yoga? The practice of meditation or prayer?
Character?

Bidding her goodbye,
I wondered if we would ever meet again.

SUMMER HAVENS

The glory days of sailing
Are past and ahead,
The cool, swift winds of Spring and Fall,
Gone and to come.
Mid-summer on the Chesapeake
With its still air, baking temperatures,
        Whiteness of sky, relentless sun,
            Little relief.
When those of light eyes, light skin
Seek protection, the haven of shade,
        Under a towering maple,
        An awning on a back porch,
        A catalpa overhanging a front porch,
        A big hat or umbrella,
Or mild relief, moving to a high spot on a hill
        Where there may be the hint of a breeze.

It is the time of cicada-song,
Of sipping cool lemonade,
Of enjoying the succulent wetness of watermelon,
Of weeding, picking beans, tomatoes, early,
        During the cool of morning;
Of quiet afternoon chores, minimal movement,
Of women husking the corn,
        Preparing the green beans for supper;
Of summer reading – Dostoyevsky, Merton, Twain
        The latest 'beach read'.
The appreciation of stillness of being,
The blessedness of cloud-cover,
The hope of summer rain with its sky- splitting
        Thunder, lingering smell of ozone,
        Welcome break from the heat.
When the season turns, just a memory.

STAR HILL

It was the name of your New England house,
An old Cape with barn and shed tucked beside,
Bordered by an ancient stone wall,
The stones originally from your field.

"We mostly grow stones in our Maine fields",
        Ted used to say.

But you lived there comfortably
        At the top of a long hill,
Writing your poems as you looked out
        On the orchard,
Those spare sentences,
        Spare forms – Haiku –
        Words chosen carefully, deliberately,
That made images dance on the pages
        Of your hand-made books.
One you gave me, covered in flowered corduroy,
        So lovingly done.

On one visit, you invited us into the barn,
Allowed us to peruse the old glass, implements,
        There offered,
A small pressed glass dish, that time, a gift.
We, hungry collectors, were then invited to the shed,
Where the next-best items were displayed.
"Come again and we will visit the house".
In awe, we entered your sanctuary,
You, pointing to this desk or that table,
        Available for purchase.
When we expressed interest, a price – or,
        'No, that is going to the museum."

All so carefully boundaried,
Your life, your poems, so meticulously catalogued,
        Arranged.

You sent little love-notes in your artful hand,
        Worthy of framing;
Along with newspaper clippings, pictures of you
        At your readings.

Years later we sought you out,
Drove up the long hill,
The house empty…
Like a wound.

FEVER

Italian men! –
Especially young men of the city,
Dressed to kill –
Tight pants
Fitted jackets
Of exquisite cloth.
Men of dark hair, eyes,
An eyebrow raised in sweet collusion,
Or arms opened wide in welcome,
An inclusive embrace.

Men who love speed,
Ferraris, Lamborghinis, Fiats,
Who flash by on the highway,
Or on the smallest roads;
Who, in Rome, aggressively drive into a circle,
One hand on the wheel,
Other hand out the open window
Prepared to strike the side of the car,
While shouting at drivers
In their way;

Who, in Venice drive water taxis
With exuberance,
Darting expertly, hair-raisingly, in and out
Of the wakes of other boats,
Other traffic, fearing nothing;
Who seize life – and their women – with gusto.

One young pony-tailed man, waiting in a line,
Tried for a kiss from his girlfriend,
She, pulling back, refusing.
He, looking annoyed, insistent,
        Not to be rebuffed,
        Moved in for a long, deep embrace,
            Then, away in triumph, eyeing his prize.

Oh, the life in it,
        The burning of it!

LIFE

THE CIRCLE

Two couples entered the elevator.
The younger, stood close together,
She, petite,
He, a head taller, strongly built.
She laid her head back against his chest,
Relaxed after sunbathing.
He held her carefully,
The older couple looking on,
Perhaps his parents.
His eyes softened,
Looking down on his bride,
And he, gently, so gently,
Blew on her hair –
They, in their own world,
Drawing us all into their circle of love.

RESTING PLACE

"I want to die here", said our friend.
He has come to this lovely place to look for a house,
Where we, too, have a home.
"It is quiet here", he continued. "I like that".
But there is more to it, it seems.
He has been coming here from time to time for years
To visit, play golf, enjoy the warmth and sun.
He has friends here –
People with whom he does business,
People with whom he plays golf,
Who have witnessed his hole- in-one,
The first, on that particular green,
On a special and difficult course.
They feted him, toasted him with champagne.
He is known within that circle
For this feat.

Perhaps this is what any of us desires,
A place where we can be comfortable,
Where we are known and appreciated,
Where we have made a mark,
A place where we would choose
To end our days,
Quiet, content.

MARTY

Her face is like a roadmap –
Or the stitching on the quilts she makes –
        a Crazy Quilt.
When she smiles, as she does frequently,
All the roads change direction,
        The stitching re-arranges itself.
An instant friend to all, she strikes up conversations
With perfect strangers,
        Engaging them,
        Drawing them into her orb,
        Sharing her impressions of a painting, a food,
        Inviting theirs.
We discover that we are sisters, in the same college sorority,
        Though some years and distance apart…
            But linked.

Her beauty, her light, emanates from inside.
She makes one feel comfortable,
        Valued,
        Part of the Family of Man,
        Glad to be so.

My friend Marty.

AWE

Lying on that beach in Maine,
Sand scratchy-hard beneath our heads,
You wondered at the pin-points
    In the night sky,
    The vastness.
We, so young,
Feeling like we understood all,
Had many worlds to conquer,
More languages to learn,
Countries to explore,
A lifetime ahead –
Austria in the Fall, working on your German,
Then on to Lebanon…
Bursting with naïve energy,
Feeling unlimited, expansive.

I remember the sudden recognition
Of just how small we were,
Two souls careening through the universe
On this tiny planet,
…and were left speechless.

A DRINK - OR DRINKS

Parched,
So thirsty.
In such a state, nothing is so welcome,
so refreshing,
as a glass of water,
iced tea, lemonade,
a lovely, cool drink.

'Come for drinks', on the other hand,
a wholly different connotation –
end of the afternoon, early evening,
something alcoholic, most likely,
pleasant conversation,
perhaps a little louder, gayer,
as time passes,
the guests imbibe.

What a difference an 's' can make.

CAFÉ MOCHA

It was a delicious indulgence,
Warm, sweet, frothy.
Sleepy when I began to drink it,
I gradually perked up…
Just the intended effect
On that lazy afternoon.

All the while, I knew,
Come three a.m.
I would join other insomniacs,
Reaching for warm milk,
Reading a book,
Looking out at the night sky
Waiting for sleep.

KINDNESS

"My father died when I was young.
My mother was mentally ill.
Life was unpredictable.
In high school I had an art teacher who
        Took me under her wing,
        Encouraged my talent.
She became a rock for me.
It meant everything."
Looking directly at me, she said,
"She was so kind", and the tears started.

Kindness
        To another human being
        To one alone
        To one starved for affection,
            Acknowledgment, caring...
Can transform the world.

My good friend has since been a benefit and blessing
To the lives of many, many people.
The loving energy she received
        Has multiplied many times
        For the betterment of others.
Who can anticipate the impact of our actions
        For good or ill?

CATCHING

"That conversation with my boss did not go as I expected.
He knew that I was facing a difficult situation.
I thought he would support me.
Instead, I was scolded like a naughty child.
I know you are retired, but someone suggested I call you."

As he spoke, the muscles of my jaw were tightening,
        My breath quickening,
        My mind trying to track
                What might have happened,
                What next step might be best.
As a counselor, as a human being,
I know that the best response
        Is to listen, be present to another.
A phone call like this, for counsel,
Comes less frequently now,
The discipline of keeping emotional distance,
Called on less often than when it was my work.

I realize, literally, the origin of the expression 'pain in the neck'.

And I catch myself…
        Catching the other's dis-ease.

DISCIPLINE

"I have lost my discipline.
I don't know where it has gone", she said,
As if it were a missing possession,
Her face troubled, her voice, plaintive,
As she sat in her wheel chair,
Eyebrows raised over eyes that searched
        Back and forth,
Trying to retrieve something tenuous in her mind.

How often do we feel thus?
There are moments in life when our sense of
Discipline wanes:
Following graduate school or a period of intense
Study, wishing never to have another exam, write
Another term paper or thesis;
After retirement, without the need for tightly
Scheduled days or lives;
During the 'golden years' of declining health, physical
ailments, a slower pace, less energy.

Some never develop this attribute,
Waiting for life to simply happen, watching it pass,
Hoping for a budding opportunity that never comes,
A brass ring, never caught.

But for one whose life was marked by discipline,
Whose mind was taut, sharp...
A perplexing loss.

CHALLENGE - IN YOUR EYES

It is in your eyes –
The hunger,
The anticipation,
The rising to it,
The will to win, dominate, overcome,
        Irrepressible in you.
The gauntlet has been thrown.
Game on!

GORGEOUS

"Hi, Beautiful!",
"Hello, Gorgeous!",
went the years-old greeting with a dear friend.
No need to say who was calling.
No question who would be greeting me in this way.
Long ago she had sent a birthday card
Featuring two seriously plain-looking older women,
Sitting in straight-back chairs.
Two speech-bubbles appeared over their heads:
"Happy Birthday, Beautiful!"
"Thanks, Gorgeous."

We had shared moments of crisis together,
Dealt with situations of human tragedy in our work.
Through those difficult times,
When our work was confidential,
Could be shared with no one else,
We offered each other support, and
Offered up dilemmas to One greater than
Ourselves.
All so serious.

I am thankful for humor
That enables one to move forward,
Keeping life in perspective,
Making for deep bonds.
I am thankful for my 'gorgeous' friend.

DREAM

Last night I dreamed of
Trying to organize
A cast of disparate characters,
As different as night and day,
All vying for attention,
All voicing different ideas about
        What was important,
        Who should speak first,
        How they should behave.
What a din!
I could not calm them,
        stifle or,
                control them,
Though I raised my voice, became angry
And frustrated with them.
I awakened, shaken.

Suddenly, an insight –
They just wanted to be honored,
        To be accepted, heard.
Smiling to myself, I began to say 'yes' mentally
To each of these characters,
Though the dream had ended.

Aspects of one's personality,
        Wanting some recognition.
A need met,
Peace attained,
For the moment.

HIGH SCHOOL REUNION

We search each other's eyes, face,
For a glimmer of recognition.
There are no nametags at this first reception.
Did I know you among this class numbering 437?
It has been fifty years!
One man, I did not know him well, commented,
        "Looks like a bunch of old people!"
A nearby friend retorted,
        "Have you looked in a mirror lately?"

But then there were the close friends –
Nuggets of pure gold as the old Girl Scout song went.
I'd know you anywhere…

LESSONS

At some point you realized.
You were living it again,
Same pattern, again.
Drawn to that same person,
Who may look different this time –
Male, female, dark, light,
Green eyes or blue,
But the same.

And you knew it was over.
Time to change course,
Behaviors.
Lesson learned.

SEASON

Shedding, shedding…
The ribald coats of mail, of male,
The protection of early lace, of lion's paw,
Of tender green shoots,
Prickly larches once soft as a baby's blanket,
A vulture's nest.

The copiousness of the barn with sagging roof,
        Brimming;
Great-grandmother's wooden chairs, seats, cane-less,
Scraped bare by generations of dungarees, petticoats,
Once precious, now for burning in the black of night.

Rusty implements of mysterious purpose,
Collections of bolts, screws, iron nails,
That join, link, destroy, rivet, un-hinge, decay.
Matchbook recollections – the Brown Palace,
The Georgetown Inn, Links to fine times,
Two Russians in Black, sumptuous meals,
Many pleasures.

Civil war powder horns, shot pouches, cow bells,
        Basins and ewers,
Precious mementos of ancestors, little valued by
        Those coming after.
Collected memories, soothing as soft summer,
Waning gold, heart-piercing, life summaries,
Sweet-bitter,
Sad for the joy of it, the fullness.

FAMILY

FAVORITE UNCLE

A man of smiles,
Heart of gold,
Humble, never boastful,
Always complimentary, up-building others,
Gracious, kind,
Generous of heart.
'We love you. We are proud of you',
          to his nieces.

Why, then, was my aunt so critical? –
          seemingly without end,
                    mercy,
                              feeling?
She could not bear his aging, his missteps,
          his forgetfulness.

A lack in herself? Her own fear?
Certainly, not his.

And in the end, when he predeceased,
her devotion to her partner of sixty years
          came through.
"I just want to be with Jimmy",
her only wish.

SON

He enveloped her in his two hands, held her up,
Cradled her in the crook of his arm,
His tiny three-month-old daughter,
A little mirror of his dark hair, his eyes,
All the while, conversing
With his loquacious two-year-old son,
Who vied for his father's attention,
Talking as fast as he could,
Topics ranging freely.

Later, he attempted to explain to us, his parents,
Something of his work,
The world of streaming information, images,
Soon losing us with technical vocabulary,
Concepts beyond our experience, foreign, new;
Telling of his trip to Scandinavia
To meet fellow workers face to face,
To talk through new directions for the company.

Who is this man I knew so well as a boy,
Whose language I barely understand, though I try,
Try not to seem 'out of it', antiquated?
I am the proud mother,
Not wanting to appear foolish in my admiration of
        His knowledge,
        His parenting (he never raises his voice),
        His regard for the Earth ('green' conscious),
        His size (he looks down as he gives me a hug).

It seems not long ago that he was
A child who frequently got lost, a dreamer,
Thinking of many things, his own thoughts,
His own world, not noticing
When we had parted ways;
An awkward teen, all arms and legs,
Growing in spurts,
Yet surprisingly strong, suddenly besting
His amazed older brother;
A soccer 'hero' who shunned the spotlight,
Gave up the sport,
Just as we had visions of a scholarship;
A rock-climber, of whose adventures (and mishaps)
I am still learning.

He has always gone his own way,
Thought his own thoughts,
Had an inherent link to 'spirit',
Carrying a shield (the lid of a trash can)
Emblazoned with 'Lord of Light'.

Distance now discourages frequent visits.
He is launched, however,
In the best way we knew how.
His life, now, the result of choices only he can make.

CONNECTION

How long, do you suppose, will I continue to talk to
you in my mind, even aloud, since you left nine years ago?
There is comfort in such conversations still, still…
Though they are only one-way…
A means of
        Maintaining contact,
        Expressing what I felt, feel now,
        Mulling over a decision, seeking guidance.

For the first year it was frequent.
Once in a while something would remind me of you -
        Clearing out the house,
        Doing something you also enjoyed, such as
            Gardening,
        Going to a place that you particularly liked
            In your many years of living.
Over the next few years, less often would I feel
        Prompted to speak to you.
And in recent times,
        I have thought to say a few words to you
        On only a handful of occasions,
Sometimes just to say the name I used to call you.

Strange, it has been forty-five years since I left home,
        Married, engaged in a profession,
            Reared a family,
        And in that time, our contact was infrequent –
        All the busyness,
And much distance between us.
But the emotional tie stayed strong, and remains so.
No one could have asked for a better father.

COMPANION (LOVE-OBJECT)

Sweet brown eyes,
Gazing with ultimate trust,
Unconditional love;
Ears a bit too large,
The longest nose imaginable,
But like his mother's;
Pinkish skin, so soft, a tad mottled;

He is larger then most, stands tall, solid in build.
Smart, alert, cagey at times,
Loves a good meal
In fact, eats most anything,
Vegetables, fruits, meat (his favorite) & potatoes,
Sweets (though not good for him).

He is sensitive to feelings, to the slightest change in
My voice or mood,
Right there when trouble threatens,
Ready to comfort or defend.

No one like him – my dog Tav.

WHEW!

He awoke from a dream crying.
Heavy with sleep, he sought out
        His mother, his father,
        Who were not there.
Only I, whom he barely knew.
The crying more intense now,
        He was sobbing.
"What's wrong? Did you get scared? Surprised?"
He wandered to the couch where I sat
        And muttered incoherently,
        Struggling for breath.
"Come here, sit down", I said,
        Cradling his little body in my arm.
I held him tight.
No words, just "shhh", for some minutes
        And gradually, gradually,
        He began to relax.
"Look, Grandma, here's a book about steamshovels!"

Whew!

GASTRONOMIE

Navy bean soup, lemon meringue pie,
    Poached eggs on toast…
Whenever I eat any of these foods,
    My mind flashes back to moments of
    Sharing them with my father.
The fact that one has similar likes/dislikes for certain
Foods to those of a parent seems to make sense –
The parent to whom one seems more
    Genetically linked.
His and my tastes seemed to have little in common
With the person who prepared food in our family,
    My mother, in my case.
At breakfast time, Mother would sit
    Happily munching on her cold cereal,
While my dad and I would talk about how good a
Poached egg would taste.
    She never fixed a poached egg.
    Nor was she interested.
    So he and I did.
She never baked. Nor did she care for desserts.
    But I did.
As soon as the aroma of baked goods wafted from
The oven, my dad would appear from nowhere,
    A smile on his face.
At a restaurant, if lemon meringue pie was available,
Dad and I would exchange a look,
Silently acknowledging what we knew we would be
ordering -
    A wordless 'high-five'.

On rare occasions, my mother would fix
Liver and onions for Dad and me.
She always refused to eat it.
Could not bear the smell of it.
She and my sister ate something else…
Anything else.

That link with my father, I still cherish –
Now only in memories
Prompted by my stomach.

SUSPENDED

They have opened his chest,
Opened his heart
To make a repair.

Operation, a success, they thought,
But the patient almost died when it failed.
A second operation…the same incision?
'We can pull him through…'
This was supposed to be routine…
The waiting…

In fact, the heart was weakened,
More than they knew,
The doctors shocked by its recent deterioration.
He didn't tell them that he almost killed himself
Trying to complete all the projects of the summer
In just the last few weeks,
        Around the house, pool, pond, the boat…
Perhaps the price too great?
Time to re-think priorities?
One or two too many?

Just before, he asked, "I wonder if I'll see Him?"
"Hope not, at least not for any length of time",
Says she.

Now, for the wife, time stands still.
Others' lives move forward – move somewhere –
        Move.
She, distracted, rides roller-coaster feelings,
        Unable to focus,
While he lies sedated, sustained by
        Machines, tubes, medicines.
The priest comes,
        Prayers, quietly offered.

Surely, there is more left – more life, more fun,
        More adventure – into old age – for this pair.
"It's too soon. Don't leave yet."
There are a million things to tell, to share –
"Here's a newspaper article you should see,
        A joke you would love,
        A legal decision you will not believe."

"It's too soon. Don't leave yet."

MEMORY

A memory emerges of
Two sisters and their friends,
Gathered around the radio,
Chattering, sharing popcorn,
Waiting in anticipation
For the event of the week.

A hush falls, as the announcer begins,
"Who knows what evil lurks in the hearts of men?,
The Shadow knows…"

MY DOG TAV

Your small body is a miracle of design,
You run, turning on a dime,
A sheepherder by breed.
You, unconditional love incarnate,
Your loyalty, faithfulness, devotion.
You make me feel like royalty – and
I am a fool for you, calling you every silly pet name
Imaginable.
I am blessed to have a friend so true,
There to absorb every mood,
Celebrate, play, comfort.
Watching you as you sleep, I notice the perfection
Of color, design in your furry face.

Recently, the discovery that one of your hips has
Eroded,
The muscle of your leg atrophied, a shock.
You drag your foot from time to time.
We now recognize the way you compensate,
Your increasing lameness.
People ask, "How old is he?",
The question, a surprise.
At seven, you are described as a 'senior' dog.
A lump rises in my throat when you falter,
The passage of time, too swift, infirmity, too soon.

Some day the squirrels outside will not lure you
To the chase so quickly,
Though now, you still send them running.

You will live forever, my Tav,
Embodied in flesh or memory.

INSPIRATION

It took only a moment.
"A beach towel!", you exclaimed.
You and your brother were on a scavenger hunt
Designed by your dad that took you all over
Our house and fields.
Grandpa and I tagged along.
We were all stumped by the riddle,
'What gets wetter and wetter the more it dries?'
Your dad loves riddles.
So do you.
You, with your quick mind, had the answer.
We all looked at you, amazed.
Your brother, the older one, was startled, dismayed.
"How did you know that? And so fast?"
"I don't know. It just came to me."
He is bigger, excelling in many things,
But in this case,
Your modest, but satisfied, smile said it all.

"I LOVE YOU"
(For My Sister)

Why did it take us so long?
About 65 years, it seems.
Why the reluctance?
        The self-consciousness?
        The embarrassment?
Not something that came easily in our family,
Expressing deep feelings.
Just three words, but how they
        Break down walls,
        Open up hearts,
        Heal.

WHY?

So young and too soon
You died, they said.
But there had been worlds
In that living,
Many lives, many lifetimes,
Too much knowing,
Time spinning by,
Blurred by chemicals of choice at the moment,
Heightened to beyond reality,
Or perhaps the only reality possible.
Part genes, part soul, part the growing up,
        Abandoned, alone,

Gathering all within that gifted sway,
A force to be reckoned with, but lost,
Reaching, searching, for something,

For meaning.
Was there meaning?
Pain, yes, innocence early and
Beauty spent.

ALL RIGHT

I sprinkled the dirt,
"Dust to dust".
"Is it alright? What do you think?"
My son lifted the box,
Placed it in its resting place,
Your son, there,
        but not there.
It is all right.

MEMORY-MAKING

This room, so full of memories,
Each item, a trigger.
The carpet, bought from a trusted merchant,
So loved, the moment we saw it,
Eyed by someone else,
Our friendly dealer guiding them
In another direction, while
Smiling across the room at us.
It has been a focal point of our favorite living
Space for years.
The 'lady's chair', just my size,
One of Sue's prize pieces that,
Because we acquired it,
Did not go the 'the museum'.
The bargello pillow I made for my aunt to match
Her living room sofa,
Returned after her passing.
Grandma's cuckoo clock, now silent,
The mere sight of it, reminding me of its
Sound, marking the hours in her library,
As she sat at her desk.
The powder horn and canteen of your great, great
Grandfather, soldiering in the Union army
Until he was wounded, so long ago.

The march of generations…
The sadness for us to think that these items we
Treasure may be gone, dispersed.
The truth we acknowledge that each generation,
Builds its own memories,
Finds its own treasures which help them recall
Particular times,
Particular people
That meant something to them.

Much can be passed on,
But the memory-making, their own.

OUR SONG

'They're playing our song',
We have heard starry-eyed couples saying,
        Time and time again.
My husband and I glance at each other,
        Veterans of a forty-six year marriage.
'What was that song that was played at our wedding?
        We danced to it.'
It was a romantic tune, suggested by the band-leader,
Since we had no ideas of our own.
When it was announced, as we, the bride and groom,
        Moved to the dance floor,
The band-leader claiming it was 'our song',
        There were audible 'ah's' and 'how sweet'
From the guests.
Haven't a clue what it could have been.
We never did have a favorite song.
In my memory are a couple of other favorite songs –
        'Moon River', 'In my room'.
But these were with earlier beaus that didn't last.
My spouse and I would sooner say,
        Tchaikovsky's Piano Concerto in D minor,
        Samuel Barber's 'Adagio for Strings',
        Copeland's 'Tender Land'.

We never have danced to another's tune.

SOUL/SPIRIT

CARRYING GRACE

Grace is all around.
The Light is around and through.
Hear the birds waking to it?
The mockingbird calls in endless variety,
  Seeking the perfect song,
  A melody that expresses utter joy,
    That captures this moment,
    This Now.

We move through the day,
  From place to place,
    Meet with others,
    Carrying grace?

How to stay with this joy,
  In this Light?
    Carry it with us,
    Emanating its purity,
  Unsullied by the clutter of ego,
    Of pain, of memories
    That linger and cut?
To return to that still place,
  That higher plane
Where we know the mockingbird's joy
  From inside, out.

QUIET MIND

A quiet mind, always there,
As near as stepping next door,
As simple as deciding, wanting to be there –
And resting.
Thoughts bombard us for a time,
Past conversations,
Decisions to be made,
New ideas, creations,
Solutions to problems,
A poem.
We watch them pass like clouds,
Resist the temptation to engage,
Simply rest.
Soon, the stillness comes
The holy emptiness, the Light.
I know that Buddha smile.

What would You have me do?

CHALLENGE II

To what will you rise,
        What take on?
What is worth your effort, your energy?
Something of this world,
        Or something beyond?
What motivates you, calls you?
Plumbing the depths,
        Or another's riches?
Interior
        Or exterior territories?
What, the reward you seek,
        Earthly,
            Heavenly?
        Present,
            Eternal?

Questions for a life….

BRITTLE

You are a fragile one,
Easily hurt,
Easily broken?
Your voice falters, eyes become downcast
          When you are challenged, even mildly.

What or who has harmed you so?
A trauma when young?
A vicious older brother – or sister?
Worse?

What will set your heart soaring?
Free your spirit?
Bolster your bruised self?

May you know beauty –
Moonbeams and starlight,
The golden days of autumn,
The thrill of a perfect sail,
The courage to plunge into blue-green water,
The joy of a puppy's unconditional love,
The savoring of your own creation, well done,
Your heart's desire, discovered.

Or, perhaps, simply a moment of peace.

IN AND OUT

Slipping in and out of Grace
in and out of You
of It
of Him

I meet new people
I am
tied to your heart…your soul
to Your heart…Your soul
His heart…His soul
You tie us together
We are connected through You.

I forget,
down I drop
into fear, competition, uncertainty.
Remembering, I am part of the We
I am
lifted, embraced, embracing.

Leave the door open, my soul.

GIFT

Each poem is a gift, beloved,
A gift of quiet, of slowing,
        of drifting, contemplation.
A gift born out of silence,
A gift from the Beloved to the poet,
        the reader.

Poetry makes a space in time,
        a different quality of time,
        within which one can rest,
                be.

For this,
        I am
        grateful.